David Matless

# The Regional Book

*Uniformbooks* 2015

First published 2015
Copyright © David Matless
ISBN 978-1-910010-05-1

*Uniformbooks*
7 Hillhead Terrace, Axminster, Devon EX13 5JL
www.uniformbooks.co.uk

Trade distribution in the UK by Central Books
www.centralbooks.com

Printed and bound by T J International, Padstow, Cornwall

Force yourself to see more flatly.
—Georges Perec, *Species of Spaces* (1974)

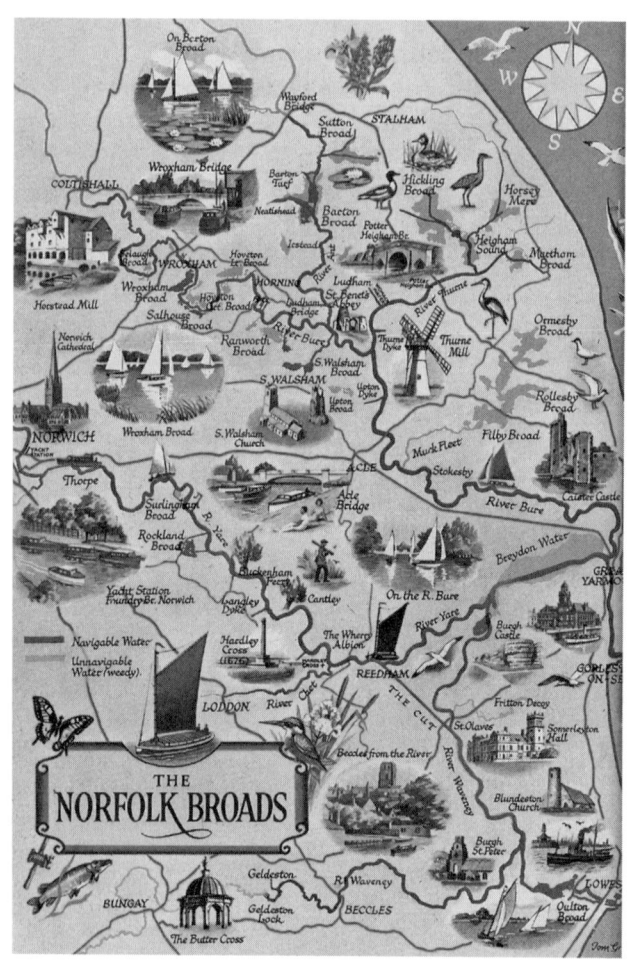

Map of the Norfolk Broads, from Eric Fowler, *Broadland in Colour* (Jarrold, 1970)

THE REGIONAL BOOK

## *Geographical Description: The Broads*

"...rivers spread over East Norfolk and Suffolk like your right hand held palm upwards. The Thurne is the thumb, and the fingers are the Ant, Bure, Yare and Waveney. They make a handful of waterways all joining one arm where it runs into the sea at Yarmouth."
—John May, *The Norfolk Broads Holiday Book and Pocket Pilot* (1952)

This *Regional Book* gathers forty-four pieces of geographical description, of sites within the Broads, a wetland area of eastern England. All are mapped on the Ordnance Survey's Landranger Sheet 134, all are publically accessible.

The broads are shallow lakes, flooded medieval peat excavations, set alongside or within the courses of the rivers Ant, Bure, Thurne, Waveney and Yare. The Broads as region includes the broads as lakes. On Broadland's 'Southern Rivers', the Yare and Waveney meet at Breydon Water, the Chet enters the Yare above Reedham, the Wensum joins below Norwich. On the 'Northern Rivers', the Ant joins the Bure, the Thurne and Bure meet, and the Bure continues, ending in the Yare below Breydon. All rivers are tidal for at least part of their course. Only the Yare keeps its name to the sea at Great Yarmouth. Scroby Sands sits offshore, marked by wind turbines.

Northern and Southern systems are gathered under the regional name of the 'Norfolk Broads', though the Waveney forms the Norfolk-Suffolk county boundary, the term 'Norfolk and Suffolk Broads' sometimes used. Broadland was 'discovered' for leisure, and for natural history, in the late 19th century. Navigation, holidays and nature conservation have shaped the region, with tensions arising from differing assumptions about what the Broads landscape has been, is and might be. The 1950s finding of the broads' artificial origin prompted concern over loss of natural value, yet also schemes to excavate new waters. Sailing and motor cruising have offered different landscape experience, with contrasting values projected; yachts tapping the elements and making for self-reliance, cruisers offering sat-back relaxation. Arthur Ransome set the two at odds in 1934 in *Coot Club*, sailing children defending birds against 'Hullabaloo' cruisers. Holiday liveliness worries those viewing Broadland as nature region.

The botanist has cherished regional flora, the ornithologist regional bird life. Binoculars, baskets, cameras, notebooks and guns have guided human attention. Reserves shelter nature from forces held to threaten, carved out by individual and institutional owners over a hundred years, wildlife maintained in trust. The late twentieth century brought diagnoses of an environment in crisis, waters clouded by eutrophication, aquatic life denuded. Grazing marshes were defended from deep arable drainage. Public authorities make efforts at ecological restoration, while an emerging climate consensus highlights future flood, with tidal surges up river more frequent, and dune breach more likely. The ends of landscape haunt the present. What might Broadland's future nature be?

This *Regional Book* takes account, examining regional cultural landscape via site description, through the Broads' varied constitution; nature reserves, towns, riversides, marshes, seasides, waterways broad and narrow, broads landlocked and connected. Past accounts can be read, readings recommended, arguments weighed, the contrasting answers to questions acknowledged, but what follows if, after all, the request is for a description? Geographical description concentrates attention, gathers experience, observes and inscribes. To account for a region, move across its varieties.

The descriptive pieces are ordered alphabetically. They practise a cross-regional democracy, with locations treated in non-hierarchical fashion, but with attention to the ways in which hierarchies (of service provision, of cultural distinction) operate. There is likewise attention to different regional objects, treating things in non-hierarchical fashion but acknowledging the ways in which hierarchies (of value, of durability, of beauty) operate. The accounts attend to landscape's complexity; its emotional and financial value, its movement across registers economic, political, cultural and aesthetic, its working through all senses, its colloquium of voices.

Works informing this *Regional Book*, whether for their regional coverage, method or aesthetic, are noted under 'Recommended Reading'. In his 1974 *Species of Spaces*, Georges Perec, outlining "practical exercises" for describing a Paris street, proposes exhaustive itemisation to take description beyond expected or conventional forms of notice. Perec states: "Force yourself to see more flatly". Perec's accounts themselves move between matters of fact, digression, memory and reverie, and show inventories to be neither plain nor simple. The injunction to "see more flatly" can however serve as a motto for constant notice, respectful looking, the spotting of unlikely material significance.

The geographical descriptions offered here cut against, while also recognising, and occasionally inhabiting, forms of attention, and styles of seeing, claiming conventional authority. If Broadland is a flat landscape, with few rises, it remains possible to see more flatly.

# 1

# Acle Straight

*The longest straight stretch of the main A47 road between Acle and Great Yarmouth*

A short straight out of Acle; so quick. A bend already, a turn off and mill sails, perhaps all done; but round the bend comes the full straight, evidence direct. Four flat miles more, any end in faint sight, without a turn. Horizon blocked by Yarmouth. North, mills mark slight Bure twists, marsh fields away. South, far towers, some sailed, some stumped. A distant pylon. Otherwise distance with nothing to lean on.

Foot down flight in straight night speed. Or a slow summer arrow to Yarmouth's back end. Traffic bound to line, crashes tending head on. Trains track parallel east. Far end fields lie deep drained arable. Another rail comes southwest diagonal. Miniature transports under sky's scope, vehicles becoming toy. Breydon closes to round things, and a bend takes the straight away.

# Barton Broad: Heron's Carr

*A nature trail boardwalk at the southern end of Barton Broad in the Ant valley*

Boardwalk opens where only science would visit. Wood succeeding reed, rooting deep mud, dykes exposing brown. Tossed coins sink, barriers and injunctions guarding temptation; just how deep, how liquid?

    A platform views north across Barton's mile, cruisers making for the Ant north or south, sound chugging over water. Waterfowl attend, crust hopeful. Black pen-on-wood lettering announces Wildlife Sightings, the box lid opening to a margarine-tubbed notebook, falling at random on kingfisher, pterodactyl, peregrine, duck. Comic flights and serious ticking. Public archival broadside.

# 3

# Belaugh

*A small village on the Bure between Coltishall and Wroxham*

Above Wroxham's rail bridge, the town stops. Trees hem, one side or either, the riverside unbuilding. A big south meander, churches oppositely banked. Curve south upstream to pass Wroxham on high to the east, the bank grassing down for a dip; bend north to pass Belaugh on high to the east.

Moor to visit St Peter, steeply upwards to the flowery yard, rarities noted. Lanes with houses branch beyond. Local scenes cushion the knees. Arcading questions dating. Common wealth unfaces painted saints.

The staithe at the northern, western turn. Properties and a lane dip to water. An iron signature in birds on green. Autumn shades glow, things are tied up.

At the south of the bend, a woodlocked broad. No river banks but trees, the Bure lent breezeless capacity. Sound channelled, the cassette playing California snow to birds and cows. Evening flights pull dark over craft.

# 4

# Berney Arms

*An isolated hamlet and railway station on the Yare at the western end of Breydon Water*

Yare and Waveney flow north and east to confluence, by Berney Arms. Boat, foot and train can take you there.
    By boat, public house mooring, various openings. A little up the Yare, seventy feet of sailed mill, former pump and grinder. Cement worked here. Current drainage is small bricked electric. Across the Yare, still Haddiscoe Island farms. Seago's Marsh reserves nature.
    Or walk from Reedham by riverbank, or by Breydon from Yarmouth; or over marshes, cow terror lurking. Longer distanced paths divide worsted and sail, routes greater than individual accomplishment. Benches carry poetic embellishment for the walker's resting, reading behind.
    Or by train, a couple stopping daily. White capitals on black metal signal the platform, for alighting, or not alighting wrong, stranded until tomorrow. Norwich points one way, Yarmouth the other, hand out to hail. Scroby blades frame a clear day east. Signs at the lone short north platform's end direct to trains. South, ex-sleepers pile before bullaces. No qualms about track walking here. Fines and death carry no deterrent. None to see, or hear.
    Travellers receive direction. Lichen crusts mill monumental signage. Noticed handwriting gives inn's delights. Standard posters trumpet London magic to frequenters of nowhere.

# Breydon Water: North Shore

*The north side of the estuary inland from Great Yarmouth*

Yare's broadening, an estuary contained. Blue and brown commingle, flats intertidal, waders tapping. Naturalists and wildfowlers co-sponsor signage. Posts channel navigation, warning stakes submerged, dodging mud grounding.

Dyke and river conjoined or aloof by pump and sluice. One capped tower stands for older drainage. Houseboat remains stave shore mud.

Trains follow Breydon west to a divide, the Reedham branch twice more touching shore. Livestock level cross. Rolling stock moves small and flatly under sky.

Yarmouth contains, outflow deflected by two miles of towned spit. Sea blades turn as if landed. Nelson and chimneys, church and rollercoaster, line sky; and sky loops back to water colour.

# Cantley

*A village on the Yare with a sugar beet processing factory*

On the B1152 to Acle, about to dip into Bure valley, factory smoke marks the south winter horizon. Sugar beet in process at Cantley, the plume from ridge roads and valleys beyond. On the A146, look north east for clouds.

The Yare downstream of Brundall between open marsh. The Yare upstream of Reedham between open marsh. Cattle, mill stumps, trains, rooks. Silos and chimneys and stores stand for miles on the flat. On the reach by Langley marshes Cantley grows, a house dwarfed, a pleasure staithe a small mooring. Eyes drawn; distracted, grabbed.

A station and yard; industrial movement. Beet trucked, once by train or wherry. Arable Norfolk in Broadland.

# Cockshoot Broad

*In the Bure valley between Horning and Ranworth, a broad isolated from the main river*

No boat to Horning Ferry inn, across the Bure from the marsh road end. Tantalising lights of an evening. Talk crosses water on still days. The southern bank makes other sound; angling shufflings, leaves and calls. Moored craft clunk piling on passing wash.

    A five minute path finds another mooring, at Cockshoot Dike. A boardwalk bridges and tracks, to Cockshoot Broad, a hide giving on water for lilies and birds. Loops take in carr.

    Notice the water. The footbridge crosses a blockage, river water cloudy, dyke and broad clear. Biomanipulative, mechanical; algae chomped, mud pumped. Boats barred. Plant life viewed in confinements. On flows the river's obscurity.

# Coltishall

*A large village at the head of navigation on the Bure*

Going up the Bure as far as can be gone. Pass properties of substance, view the Rising Sun in the west. Navigation's social head. A staithe stretches out to wait. Common grass invites rest and play. Sitters water-gaze to an unbuilt bank. Things gather to a picture by a B-road.

    Upstream, backwaters bend right forked to a navigational end. Twenty years ago, lingering disuse made an old painting from these parts, all tree banks, leans-to and wood wrinkles. Now newer gates lock neat closure.

# 9

# Gorleston: Yare Mouth

*The mouth of the River Yare at Great Yarmouth harbour*

Best view the harbour from the Gorleston side. Fine sand beaches the pier's south, the Yare's swirling mouth washing north. Swimmers trying a crossing are hauled out, if lucky. A choppy entrance always awkward; Yarmouth's new beach outer harbour grasps for larger trade. Harbour strollers access Gorleston only, short stepping from the Floral Hall.

Inbound water turns right under brick lighthouse oversight. Sea to river, industrial quays to Haven Bridge, drifters and herring long gone, gas and wind come.

Suffolk south over a coastal rise, to Lowestoft's locked regional exit. Remembrance of late rail. Tracks to memorial corn.

Broadland waters meet the sea. Rains from Horsey and Coltishall, Norwich and Bungay, all run here. Regional silt on ebb and flow to Scroby.

# Great Yarmouth: Sea Front

*The promenade at Norfolk's largest seaside resort*

Glance sideways at the biggest dip. A glimpse of Breydon, before the screaming hurtle to Pleasure Beach ground.

Broad paving promenades north, to piers and pools, games calm and crazy, spillages of amusement. Wellington and Britannia shelter ghost varieties, stage coarser variants. Merrivale models town and country, small pleasures from giant angles. Snails roam Joyland.

A step to soft sand stops firm promenading. Effort of traction and comfort of sitting; wind broken, castles aslump. Ships in roads, turbines on banks. A boat close inshore picks people for seals.

Scroby excursions view the land; the spit's line, from harbour to Nelson, Hippodrome and pier, bedding into north denes, the Bure not a mile behind. Inland's narrow guard. California rises low. Sight stretches to a northern ness, turning to Thurne's coast. A southern ness pokes England as east as east can go.

# Great Yarmouth: Patterson Close

*A cul-de-sac in Great Yarmouth*

The sign marks the common haunt of residents. The footbridge from Vauxhall and a main road crossing finds it, the river and Breydon not far. Patterson Close, for Arthur, autodidact naturalist, observer of things common and strange.

    White capitals on green, with white trim, seven bolts between letters and trim top and bottom. Signs fixed each side of two grey two foot metal posts. Paint peeled to rust at bases. Looking from the yellow-lined gutter, a lean left of five degrees. Variation in levels of sign and post top suggests barging, human or vehicle, rather than sinking. Verge grass worn around the left post, pavement feet straying. On the left post, below the sign, a sticker for dog clean-up. A lamppost three feet from the right post, perpendicular: choice of facilities. Canine visits likely. Spiders web between metal; two signs make a sheltered trap. Passerines land at a pinch.

# Great Yarmouth: Vauxhall Station

*The only remaining railway station in Great Yarmouth, near the east end of Breydon Water*

What would have been expresses would terminate. Platforms stretch out old extents, outsizing present carriage. A decent stroll, waiting for something shorter. Retail turns the siding round the clock.

Sleepers grass beyond the central lines. A fall of use greens the edge. Two lines diesel plants away, two platforms well-trod. Yellow lines warn peril, as trains crawl by to workaday buffers. Nothing rushes to the terminus.

Holiday remnants mill in season, part-thronging the hall. Returns to the sea. Mile walkers to the front cross the Bure's last reach, footbridge planks in iron curves, Breydon glimpsed. A grander rust marks a lost dock tramway.

By the bridge, a black sheet steel curve, sail-shaped for a trading wherry, waymarking paths to out-of-town. The wood-benched brick base prospects the Bure south; metal railings and brick warehousing, cash and carry trader sales. Look north for crash barriers, forecourt taxis, low brick and white fascia. 1959's remodel lives, just.

13

# Halvergate Marshes

*The marshland between the lower reaches of the Bure and Yare, crossed by the Acle Straight*

Halvergate lends a label for marshes between Bure, Yare and the forty foot western upland. Roads cross edges, parts carry proximate or distant parish names; Tunstall, Wickhampton, Halvergate, Reedham, Berney, Beighton, South Walsham, Acle. Arable conversion at the north east proceeded no further, a green cause célèbre putting a stop, a deep drainage future deflected. Cattle browse.

Water managed for a level, a system sluiced and dyked, stations pumping to and fro rivers. Insects, some of whose names you may know, sit on dyke waters. Plants, some of whose names you may know, root sheltered. Drainage makes a choice ecology.

Try walking straight and you will deviate. Drainage intricacy takes the stroller awry. Bullocks scrutinise. Waymarkings channel walkercourses through all-year green.

# Hickling

*A village and broad on the upper Thurne*

A straggled place, from broadside wood to sea earshot. North the road bends by mill tower to church, a decent trek from parish staithe moorings. Ditches bear the lanes beyond. Past priory ruins, a flat to the dunes. Marsh wood shelters the strangest of graves.

Lanes east head to mill remains; lanes off lanes rut for seclusion. South, trust maintains reserve, choosing the succession. Wood munched or released, landscape styled for species. Cross marsh to circle luxury thatch, at the broad's edge hide. Water trails take narrow parts, instruct the unknowing, step ashore for tower views, over the canopy out to sea.

Chugging from Heigham, enter the open, passing estate life, avoiding the yachts. Putter by posts through the regional broadest, curving right north to a pleasure boat rest.

Undeep waters carry a hint of salt, a hint of tide. Breadth throws surf and dinghy sail across. Angle the shallows; capsize to stand still.

# Horning

*A village on the Bure*

Upstream from the Ferry Inn to the west end, northern banks are well appointed. Property as substantial as can be, hard by water, looking across to trees, south bank carr. Public space intrudes awhile at a sharp bend, the Swan Inn and staithe, small grass and moorings.

Parked up, a paddle boat. Cruises leave for Ranworth, spring through fall, incongruous platform for spying wet woodland. Light refreshment and waterborne licence, Mississippi-on-Bure. Jazz swings, a sailor tacks away. Loons display in bobbing wash, blithe to ragtime. A local habitation, use multiple, indifference virtuous.

# Horsey: Bramble Hill

*On the coastal dunes between Sea Palling and Winterton*

Over marsh, from mere to dune, turning right to remotest coast. Sea held by sandhills held by marram. Pass beach seals and naturists, and just before the Bramble Hill Gap cross the Horsey-Somerton parish boundary, finding the sea at the old Hundred Stream outflow. No sign now. Groynes hold the beach, plaques in Gaps report parliamentarians unveiling wall reinforcements, the coastal line held.

    The dune height sees from Happisburgh to Winterton, lights north and south, out over sea and in over marsh, the 1938 flood land and Martham's heights. Dunes run taut across a possible bay. Marsh waters head strangely inland, the coast a watershed. A fence at an angle runs the parish line, doglegging to the Sock Drain and the Hundred Stream, into the Thurne. A summer ditch puddle marks a source of sorts, water looking to Yarmouth.

# Horsey: Mere and Village

*A village and broad on the upper Thurne, close to the coast*

No boats in winter: birds only. Otherwise birds share. From Meadow Dyke narrows, out to wide water; circumnavigate avoiding weed, warily probe the Waxham Cut. From choppy mere water, look to the dunes and consider sea waves. Archaic boat houses front reed, nestle half sunk, cushioned by beds. A channel cuts to Horsey staithe, straight to a ninety degree right turn, a short end to a full sailed mill.

The estate of an old marsh island. Bank paths circle, slightest rises giving an angle on marsh and mere. Swan disks signal wires, air diversions. By the Cut, Brograve sails tilt and list. Devilish stories accrue to a brick wood sentinel.

Circle to the church by the hall, tree sheltered. A simple stone by the door marks one previous owner. Essex, Geneva, Horsey. A past in league, a present in trust. Church thatch watertight, the underside inside. Guard against an island return; Horsey dry, and just high, in a sea flood surround.

# Hoveton Great Broad

*An isolated broad and nature trail in the Bure valley, between Wroxham and Horning*

Aromatic, a broad and carr reserve gained only by water, a small Bure north bank quay. Tree and fen bar land access. Tie up and take the boardwalk, a sleeper path of half a mile, looping from entrance to exit, single file. Visits elective, no stray humans. Public authority trails nature, national reserve maintained. The warden has a hut.

Signs warn not to stray, muddy danger lurking. Experience sensibly channelled. Hides give on the broad, free of navigation, birds undisturbed. Mud accumulates shallows. Chained binoculars see terns, platform nesting. Coot graze. Kingfisher darts.

Petrol engines made this grow. Hay lost horse demand, and cutting ended. Signs mark succession, and intervention, deflecting for sedge. Numbered posts match guiding text, for moss and fern, peat solid and thin, turf ponds and the greater broad. Bird life passes by, or perches. Branches frame a sunlit tawny.

Boat noise fades into wood, traffic forgotten. River water nose drops, carr scent rising. The fruits of damp, sweet gale of fen. Currant, wild. Reserve confinements, aromatic.

# How Hill

*A house and estate on the Ant between Barton Broad and Ludham*

On a rise above the Ant, a substantial house, south facing for the sun, sheltered from a north wind, taking in the valley. Portals owner-architect inscribed: ETB 1904 Feb was here. Strapwork and pargeting, roughcast and thatch. Step from sun parlour to polite lawn, into hedged Edwardian yew topiary.

A hundred years a model estate. Water gardens nurture exotics, counter prevailing floral grain. By the river, restored mills of unusual type, once marsh pumps. Cut reeds stacked to go. Electric boats carry silent tours through narrow waters, to hides and beds. A marsh cottage restored, for viewing; eel tools, dampness. Painting classes by water. Education, propriety, the sustainable. We continue to manage.

Forty years ago, visiting to play at cricket on the neat grass. Young excitement, the Broads of no interest.

Twenty-five years ago, an elderly gent on his young estate life, the family car coming home from the city, seeing its lights the only lights across the marsh.

# How Hill: Boardwalk

*A boardwalk trail to Crome's Broad on the How Hill estate*

Paths cross marsh, pass ditches and sluices, ponies and scrapes, skirt field study privacy, reaching a boardwalk. Land too wet to walk. A diversion finds a hide, viewing Crome's Broad. Reed and tree green water waver, exotics intrude the southern end. Floor slat gaps spy water.

Outside the hide, fencing screens the broad. Carr woodland lines the path, and as the boardwalk turns right, a stick protrudes from mud. A metal marker shows a spade sign for a trail guide. The peat crust removed for two feet, the stick pokes the hole. Grasp the end and push, and then pull up, smooth sliding ten feet. Liquid mud, barely an effort. Only the held top shows bark; lumpy brown coats the rest. All this just under, the wood's weight in balance.

Tread the boards, do not stray.

# 21

# Irstead

*A small village on the Ant between Barton Broad and Ludham*

Leave Barton south for pleasant shoals; narrows unpiled, gravelly beds. As if a typical lowland river had found its way.

Irstead's green staithe, with launch dyke indented. Grass trimmed, gravel edging the mooring. No muddy landings. Boats tuck in from the main stream, room left to pass. All tied up neatly. Space for child's play, and to run dogs tightly. All fine if all is fine.

Barriers block private moorings at piles of substance. Back of the green, outdoor shelves offer scenic ceramics. Bargain bags of horse sit beside.

The church proximate, travel's patron painted. Chancel stalls rudely carved: 1663. Some further restorations. Pew-end dogs, shined from stroking, sit up and beg, rest tourer hands.

# 22 Loddon and the Chet

*A large village at the head of navigation on the Chet*

At the Yare-Chet corner, on the upstream side, Hardley Cross marks Norwich's old river reach; toll fights with Yarmouth, riparian stakes. Inscriptions list mending, reparata tempore. Spiked rails protect the lonely cross.

Turn up the Chet. Boats would not run but for digging and banking. Navigation lapsed and restored; 1884 cargo, 1958 pleasure. A small river threatens to spill, banks remade to steady flow, Chet kept in channel. Hardley Flood borders north for a mile, taking surplus, drawing birds. Peer from galley over reed and bank for glimpses; or canopy stand, gingerly surveying.

Loddon marks the head; waterfront and staithe, church and perambulation, small town affairs. Note Tayler and Green's modest modern, and the slaughter of sweet William. Some damage unmended.

## Meadow Dyke

*A narrow part of the upper Thurne, connecting Heigham Sound and Horsey Mere*

From sound to mere: following posts into narrows, water lapping as engine chugs, slow wash into reed and bank, trees made out from one another, occasional isolated halts, perching aloft to spy rare spots, winding so little ahead can be seen, surprising appearance of otherway craft, sailing with barely a width worth a tack, concentrating on the steer, passing invisible minor broads, greeting a winter Eurobird sign; relax to a mere's breadth.

# Muck Fleet

*The formerly navigable waterway connecting the Bure and Filby Broad*

Off the A1064 along the 'New Road', not on the 1910 map but there by 1932, running straight to Stokesby with one bend, over Bure marshes grazed and cropped. You might miss the Muck Fleet. White painted metal railings mark a bridge, the road barely rising over something once sailed.

One hundred years an ex-navigation; to think boats came this way, making for the Trinity Broads, now out of circulation. Above the bridge, a sluice backs a pool, weed green. Below the bridge, plant life overgrows. Railing signs state Canoeing Prohibited; somebody must have tried, injunctions warning the intrepid. A minor road crosses a dyke, road navigating over river.

# New Cut

*A canal cut between the Yare at Reedham and the Waveney at St Olaves*

From Reedham east, fork right, straight on south east, to a canal, cut to the Waveney, new just before Victoria. In a region of winding waters: something straight. An elevated marshland passage, above ditches.

Joining Norwich to Lowestoft's sea, a Yarmouth bypass. Smooth passage free of tolls: Norwich a Port! Navigational dreams outrun by trains.

The north bank carries a farm track. Stop and step onto The Island. A farmhouse passed: what a place to dwell. And one other: neighbourliness on a level.

The south bank carries rail, units from tiny distance passing small, moving south to Haddiscoe, or north curving to Yare's swing crossing. Passage beaten regular under sky.

Power lines rise to sky slim pylons, leaping cut and rail, avoiding masts. The A143 flies in concrete, in low slung modernity, a childhood spectacle to trump a ferry.

Exiting south, a bridge pier in the stream, and five in reedy marsh, marks another line's wreck. Wood blocks the old Yarmouth way.

# Norwich: Carrow Bridge

*The bridge carrying Carrow Road over the Wensum, south-east of Norwich city centre*

In the window of the control room, one white ring, stamped G.Y.P & H.C.: Great Yarmouth Port and Haven Commissioners. Lifesaving remains of old navigational rule, Carrow Bridge a pivot. Lettering speaks.

Vessels move to the port of Norwich, Carrow open for regular passage. Wharves up and down the stream; mills and plants, flour and mustard. River trade drops, mills turn to flats, bridge joints stiff now. One prolonged blast, and five short, will alert.

Boom tower ruins at the River End. Warning lights seldom flash. Cars navigate inner links. Thousands cross fortnightly, roughly, in season, for sport. Foot treads echo, the road over air, slight bounce with the numbers. Joints limber a little.

Wensum shifts a little daily, Yare's mouth registering.

# Norwich: Castle Museum

*The main museum of Norwich, in the Norman Castle in the city centre*

Ten miles from the Bure, one from the Wensum, on a Norman mound. The region on display in paint and diorama.

Galleries show once private pictures, dried two hundred years. Rivers rendered, seldom broads. Trade passage in paint, working water and wind, pump and wherry; and occasional frolics. Abbey ruins with their modern mill, but otherwise Yare dominant; Norwich a market, Yarmouth also. Detail caught; leaves growing this way, light reflecting that. A sort of regional property. Sail takes a breeze, sun and moon set composition. A Norwich river afternoon: the skill for such ease. Studies in landscape, Langley's scrutiny: uninventable.

Step to the Norfolk Room. Six county dioramas, three regional subjects. Models and backdrops, vivid arrangement. Birds autumn on Breydon, snow coats the Yare, Hickling's Broadland summers. Posts recede, background water freezes, birds pick through reed. Wigeon flight, otter glare, bittern stretch. Press buttons for avian sound. Breydon and Yare at 13 feet across, Broadland at 26; the viewer walks the field of vision, becoming naturalist. Landscape to urban indoors, taxidermy to still life.

# Norwich: Yacht Station

*The yacht station of Norwich on the Wensum, east of the city centre*

Broadland's seventh river, scarcely mentioned in the guides. The Wensum, coming all the way from Fakenham, meets the Yare above Thorpe, and drops its name. London passengers would alight at Norwich's Thorpe Station, just by the Wensum, to join another train for Wroxham, or Yarmouth; the city river sidestepped, a Broadland dead end.

Excursion boats pass the city's backs, or head downstream for scenery; woods at Bramerton, Yare's finery. No hire craft beyond Bishopbridge, where Kett crossed to take the city. Private school meadows frame cathedral prospects. 1912 rain spilled the Wensum through August streets. Late summer Saturday green and yellow passes the moored, downstream to Carrow. Distant cheers fill open canopies at the head of navigation.

# Oulton Broad

*A large village and broad inland from Lowestoft, off the Waveney*

Oulton Dyke going upstream south from a quiet stretch, skiing permitted, of Waveney. Into Suffolk, following the train, turning past wood. Cut to a suburban pond.
All but the south west built; boatyard and yacht station, motor boat club and residence. Park off the main street, keeping banks open: the public facility of looking. Lowestoft's museum remembers, by a bandstand. Tennis, trampolines, bowls. The L & OBMBC clock oversees water, hands joining round a pennant. Wide slipways permit 6 mph, a regional maximum.
Maxima exceeded every seventh summer evening, when speedboats meet. Water carved in turning, bounced in straights. Thursday viewings of Broadland sport from Everitt Park, charged. Standard boat sound eclipsed, roaring speed.
River trips depart west, Mutford Lock ends the broad east. To make Norwich a port, an old new sea link. Through road and rail bridges to Lake Lothing, middle earthly industrial water. Lowestoft harbour further. The bridge tower cons lock strollers, tannoys warning. Craft wanting beyond the lock-free and wave-free pass.

# Potter Heigham

*A village on the Thurne*

For a mile the banks lined with chalets, one deep between river and marsh. The Thurne a front garden to cruise, noting variations in chalet form, standard shed to quirky mill stump, a veranda or a lawn, fishing spot or private mooring. The river as lounge. After a mile a modern boatyard tower, a basin of cruisers for hire, a tight bridge arch ahead, medieval stone. Aim and duck. A high road bridge bypasses where rail ran. Chalets further on the rond.

Traffic lights over the hump, into riverside Potter Heigham, the village proper a distance on. Busy Saturdays in season; boat turnover, day hire, ices. Year round callers for local bargains; clothing, provisions, souvenirs, maggots.

Towards the staithe, a sign for the village; bench-circled, shop-worn and mended, with carved scenes and history words. Spandrels of heron and bittern. The old bridge and packhorse, Roman potters, reed boats, mill, yachts, cruiser, angler. Smocked and booted, a figure cuts cracked green and yellow paint, stacked medieval peat grey rendered behind. Warmth and power. Broads origins accounted.

# Ranworth

*A village and broad in the Bure valley*

Two ways to reach Ranworth Church; by car to park by the churchyard gate, or on foot from water. From Malthouse Broad moorings, a quarter mile lane, west up a gentle rise. By car you might arrive without viewing a broad.

Into the church to an open stone floor, the holy end right beyond a painted saints screen. Across the floor another door and spiral stairwell, stone inside the tower, moving by ladders through the belfry towards the top, and a narrow hatch.

To a rare airy prospect. Onto something unexpected (boats!), or something just seen (boats). Fields, fruit trees in line, and in the far east water towers and turbines; some in the sea. South, in season, factory smoke. The city south west, seven miles out of sight. Leaning over low railings to graves, tilting slightly back with perspective. West Malthouse Broad with boats, north Ranworth Broad without; with thatched, floating, conservation centre. Where the two join, a straight dyke cuts to the Bure. East a huddle of ex-abbey; walls, some tower. Modest landmarks. The valley west and north east thick wooded, further east open to marsh. Sails evident over the flat; yachts and mills. Rare perspective in the region.

# Reedham

*A village on the Yare*

The train from Norwich stops, a proper station at the edge of a village barely seen. Moving on past few buildings in cuttings, off left a line goes across marsh to Yarmouth, the Lowestoft line curving right. An empty cutting heads back left to the other branch, then under a bridge and some building backs and out to bridge a surprise of wide expanse.

The Yare swing bridge, open for rare sea coasters and high masts, with its flags and operatives, viewing riverside Reedham; a quay and moorings, green and housing. The tidal Yare takes the slack of rope; cruisers wake at a different level. Boats run away with themselves approaching on the flow.

The line continuing, curving left, gaining the bank of the straight New Cut, to Haddiscoe and the furthest east of England.

# Reedham Ferry

*A chain ferry crossing the Yare upstream of Reedham*

Two bends up from the swing bridge, the last chain ferry, saving miles for a fee. Back and forth, three cars a time, till ten the year round. Summer mornings, winter nights. Inn and tents close by.
  Narrow flat marsh roads approach, make final turns to slipways. Ring to call if the other side: One Short Peal Is Sufficient. The ferry clanks over, chains both ends, ramps up, curving against ebb or flow. Dip and climb on board according to tide. Just time to leave cars, if preferred. Cyclists Must Dismount. Cruisers up and down pause for the passage: Caution Chains.
  Curving clanking, finding the opposite slip. Prepare to drive, or pedal. Start and depart promptly.

# Salhouse Broad

*A broad in the Bure valley between Wroxham and Horning*

Up the Bure from Horning, swing right around a southern meander. Two gaps through the south bank reach Salhouse Broad. Trees hold the slim divide. Wood lines Bure one side, Broad the other.

From Salhouse village, down Salhouse Road, park with convenience at a turn in a dip. Track into trees along the contour. Wood lines an inlet. Path dips to shore.

Equipped with mooring spots, circumference dotted, and a nice grassy southside spread. Ample end-on, relaxed reverse docking. Walk up for a Wherry tap.

Grass slopes, goose cropped, to unusual perspective, the bank the river's outer incision, rising thirty feet quickly. Dew shines the incline on late season mornings. Not a car in sound, the Castle seven miles. Gain the slope, gather to a picture.

# St Benet's Abbey

*The remains of a medieval abbey on the Bure, between the mouths of the Ant and Thurne*

Leave tarmac at Shangri La and bump across the marsh. Or moor up on the Bure, by hints of bank flint. On a low rise, abbey remains.

Low banks mark major structures, Benedictine livings to tower over the flat, commanding Ant, Bure and Thurne, demanding fish and turf, carving future broads. Surrounding small heights could not but see. The newer church stamps a cross on the rise, twenty wooden feet of claim. PEACE de-ruins atmosphere. A bishop is still an abbot.

One gatehouse arch, brick mill stump conjoined. Old painter-haunted. Tufty grass on masonry jags. Lion and warrior weathered, France and England worn. Names etch the gate, hearts of old love scratched.

Over a stile, under Gothic span, to the stump door. Enter to a brick-circled sky. Eyes bright for cloud observance: scud, glide, procession. Sharper and duller from shifts beyond; whites to greys, shiny blues, rare bright blacks. Stiff-necked reverence of weather. Exit in transfigured light.

# Stokesby

*A village on the Bure between Acle and Great Yarmouth*

Down from the Muck Fleet outflow, across from Halvergate's top end, up from the Acle Straight, where fresh can switch to salt. The end of an upland tongue. The lower reaches begin, twisting embanked to Yarmouth.

On the south horizon, beet smoke in season.

The Ferry Inn for an obvious stop. Spot it from the train; tucked behind the village. At the close of cruising, rather than keeping on. Lights move over marsh on bent approaches. Ropes need slack for tide. Barleycorn was sung.

Take in the capped mill and the Georgian. Shop and idle. Walk gloaming lanes to semaphore trees.

# Strumpshaw Fen

*A nature reserve in the Yare valley, on the north bank opposite Surlingham*

Beware of trains. Look both ways from parking, cross level for entrance. Over the tracks, spread quietly on well-marked ways. Skirt the bird centres. A million voices for nature speak low. Back-route signs urge non-member payment. No dark visits.

Diggings and scrapings draw attractions. Well-worked habitat, careful composition of view. Approach hides from the rear; ascend, enter and wait. Hatches give a broad sweep, wood contains chat and murmur. Bare eyes and lenses, tripod and elbow, see concentration. Reed curtains the protected. Bitterns star.

Trail woodland and/or fen, for preference and endurance. Cross rail twice: Strumpshaw Occupation. Accept a hand-lettered swallowtail invitation. Walk to close quarters, please feel free.

Reach the Yare. The edge of reserve, the uncontained; or differently constrained. Recall walking through holiday camp wire to the beach. Boats in motion, signs of skiing, Surlingham ditches. Variegation in space, beyond the birds.

# Thurne: Village

*A village on the Thurne, between Potter Heigham and Thurne Mouth*

The ridge road gets to sixty feet. Turn and drop steadily to Thurne, tucked by staithe and river namesake. There are facilities, and the Lion, once mural graced. Victoria lingers for posting. Dirt paths view river traffic, to Thurne Mouth and regatta turnings.

Thurne dyke divides to three, permanent branches and straight overnight. Tight for turning. Multiple shuntings, three point brilliance.

The entrance clear, even in dark, the tall tapering mill at the north side. White paint advertises. Sails extend the already high, greeting the river and marking rest. Downstream another, stockier, hails the west bank, waving full since '74. The twentieth century remade us.

# Thurne: Squint

*A hole in the tower wall in Thurne church*

Ascend from Thurne village, to St Edmund King and Martyr, church standing alone, old English patronage. Eye level on the west tower wall finds a hole; a squint or hagioscope, antique curiosity. Sight through the wall to the altar, or from inside to the marshes of Thurne and Bure, dead straight to Abbey ruins. Nodules line, flint insides on show. On grass looking in, or on the chill tower floor peering out; sightlines.

Lepers, or others barred from inside, might partake in worship by sight, if not touch or taste. And the squint might signal to St Benet's, a shining hole light across the marsh. Viewing out, land falls to Thurne's level; solids and river, marsh and walls.

A sliding wooden cover blocks the inside; once a nesting shelter, a pale egg held for years, before going. Now perspex bars the outer entry. Lavender is left, a spider corpse dangles. Slide the cover shut.

# Trinity Broads

*The broads of Filby, Rollesby and Ormesby, isolated from the main river system, north of the lower Bure*

Filby, Rollesby, Ormesby: wood-hemmed reservoirs for Yarmouth. Cut off from circulation, the Muck Fleet clogged. Trinity: sail, fish, or park up and look.

The A1064 and A149 offer passing peeps. Approaching from Caister, the 149 finds the water works right, and quickly over Rollesby Bridge, Ormesby Broad right and Rollesby left. Any boats?

Eyes draw a moment from driving. From Caister, the 1064 slows for Filby, then quickly to Filby Bridge, Ormesby Little Broad right and Filby left. Yachts out? Perhaps geese? Speed hides anything smaller.

# Wayford Bridge

*A bridge carrying the A149 over the Ant, west of Stalham*

A typical prospect, an A-road glimpse. Downhill, over and up and away on the 149. Pavements, and solid barriers, metal and concrete. Speed could swerve this sweep. Quickly cross the top of a valley, noticing a waterway.

Ample parking for the Ant. Downstream mooring and boatyards, and a little further a classical shack, all pillars and pediment. Quite the display, a front on basics.

Above, houseboats, wood brown with balconies. What used to be Flat-a-Floats. Lodge on the river, hire a patch; always sit on the same stream once.

Cruise under the span but for what? Navigation ends just up, canoes excepted. Paddle an old canal to quiet, otherwise motor back. Ample turning to passenger seat glances.

# West Somerton

*A village on the upper Thurne, beyond Martham Broad, close to the coast*

The top end of the river. Through Martham Broad, the Thurne turns to West Somerton staithe. Free mooring. Permanent boats in still weed beyond. A small green, a village sign; mill, wherry and church in black metal. Over fields the North Sea, under two miles; forceful waters. There are the dunes, just over there. The Lion, with noted double cod. Wind farmed on Blood Hills; early blades etched a skyline.

For once you can stand on the waterside, look down, and see clarity. Plants visible, greenery through wind ripples. The only Broadland spot which never clouded.

# Wheatfen

*A nature reserve in the Yare valley, between Surlingham and Rockland Broads*

A Surlingham lane, becoming a track. Dirt to park, cottages tucked in green. Apples, huts and stores. The fen card index. Free to enter; you might meet the warden, or might not.
 The Ted Ellis Nature Reserve, in family trust. Edward Augustine and Phyllis. Naturalist reserve, under heron sign. Paths conduct, weather eyes see. Summer bites.
 The Thatch gives history and flood, and Ellis in rhyme. Ink hops. Left/bereft, Wheatfen/again, weed wet and trellis. Uncorporate typography stamps distinction.
 Lilies and snails, damsel and dragon, flag and tangle. Boardwalks only so far, to peter to tracks, to Broad and Deep Waters. Robin and loosestrife. Summer's path of numbered posts finds the Yare, wide passing, winter prone to surge. Tides run here. The Home Dyke gauge marked red waist high; the daily imperceptible lap.

# Wroxham

*A large village on the upper Bure*

Low loaders divert, warned of a ground base. A supplemented hump of a bridge joins boatyard Wroxham south and retail Hoveton north, home lands further each way, the downstream Bure bungalow trim. A waterside hotel speaks modest modern. Pleasure first gained purchase here, Broadland found beyond itself. Assonance of water and wallet:

> The Broad and the yacht club
> The bridge and the ducks
> Leafier avenues
> Tour boats deluxe
>
> Swanning and ducking
> Of varying class
> Here for duration
> Or making a pass
>
> Fortnights of boat hire
> In warm summer rain
> Risk family dampness
> And boredom and pain
>
> So for choice of cagoule
> Or selection of toys
> Whatever you want
> You can find it in Roys

THE REGIONAL BOOK

## Recommended Reading

Italo Calvino, *Mr Palomar* (1985)
Mark Cocker, *Crow Country* (2007)
Tim Dee, *Four Fields* (2013)
Richard Denyer, *Still Waters* (1989)
W. A. Dutt, *The Norfolk Broads* (1903)
E. A. Ellis, *The Broads* (1965)
Martin George, *The Land Use, Ecology and Conservation of Broadland* (1992)
J. M. Lambert, J. N. Jennings, C. T. Smith, Charles Green & J. N. Hutchinson, *The Making of the Broads* (1960)
R. F. Langley, *Journals* (2006)
David Matless, *In the Nature of Landscape: Cultural Geography on the Norfolk Broads* (2014)
Brian Moss, *The Broads* (2001)
R. H. Mottram, *The Broads* (1952)
Ordnance Survey Landranger Map, Sheet 134
Jason Orton & Ken Worpole, *The New English Landscape* (2013)
Arthur Patterson, *Nature in Eastern Norfolk* (1905)
Georges Perec, *Species of Spaces and Other Pieces* (1997)
—— *An Attempt at Exhausting a Place in Paris* (2010)
Nikolaus Pevsner & Bill Wilson, *Norfolk I: Norwich and North-East* (1997)
Arthur Ransome, *Coot Club* (1934)
E. L. Turner, *Broadland Birds* (1924)
Tom Williamson, *The Norfolk Broads: A Landscape History* (1997)

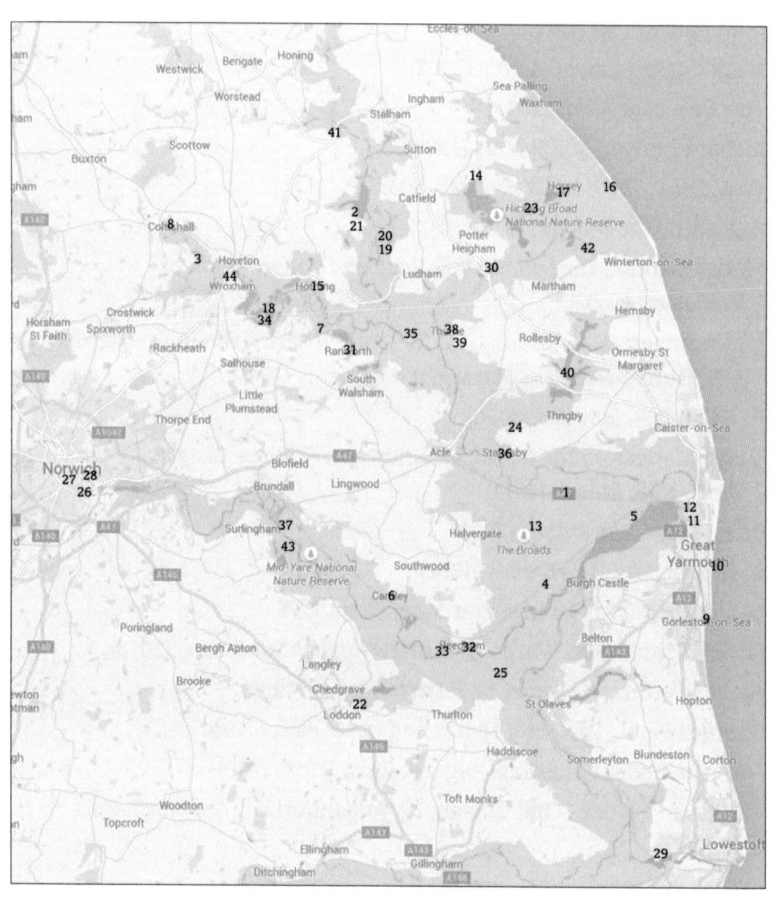

THE REGIONAL BOOK

# Gazetteer

1. Acle Straight
2. Barton Broad: Heron's Carr
3. Belaugh
4. Berney Arms
5. Breydon Water: North Shore
6. Cantley
7. Cockshoot Broad
8. Coltishall
9. Gorleston: Yare Mouth
10. Great Yarmouth: Sea Front
11. —— Patterson Close
12. —— Vauxhall Station
13. Halvergate Marshes
14. Hickling
15. Horning
16. Horsey: Bramble Hill
17. —— Mere and Village
18. Hoveton Great Broad
19. How Hill
20. —— Boardwalk
21. Irstead
22. Loddon and the Chet
23. Meadow Dyke
24. Muck Fleet
25. New Cut
26. Norwich: Carrow Bridge
27. —— Castle Museum
28. —— Yacht Station
29. Oulton Broad
30. Potter Heigham
31. Ranworth
32. Reedham
33. Reedham Ferry
34. Salhouse Broad
35. St Benet's Abbey
36. Stokesby
37. Strumpshaw Fen
38. Thurne
39. —— Squint
40. Trinity Broads
41. Wayford Bridge
42. West Somerton
43. Wheatfen
44. Wroxham